In Such Wonder

poems by

Jonel Sallee

Finishing Line Press
Georgetown, Kentucky

In Such Wonder

ACKNOWLEDGMENTS

Earlier versions of "Emissaries" and "Musings on the Cinque Terre" previously appeared in *Coming of Age: Writing & Art by Kentucky Women over 60*, Vol. 2 (Red Lick Valley Press, 2023).
An early version of "Thinking of Abraham" appeared in *&Grace* (anthology of *Lexington Poetry Month*, 2015, Accents Publishing).
"Time Travel i" appeared in the anthology of *Lexington Poetry Month*, 2023)
"Station 6," "Time Travel i," and "Time Travel ii" were posted on the *Lexington Poetry Month* website during June, 2023.

My special thanks to Carole Johnston and Normandi Ellis for their years of encouragement and friendship.

Publisher: Leah Huete de Maines
Editor: Christen Kincaid
Cover Art: Jonel Sallee
Author Photo: Holifield Photography, Lexington, Kentucky
Cover Design: Elizabeth Maines McCleavy

Order online: www.finishinglinepress.com
also available on amazon.com

Author inquiries and mail orders:
Finishing Line Press
PO Box 1626
Georgetown, Kentucky 40324
USA

Contents

Widenings 1

Our Stories 2

Melville's Study 3

A Daydream of Geese and Angels 4

Emissaries 5

Station 6 6

Suite in a Light Key 7

Matters of Light 9

Convergence 11

Time Travels i 12

Time Travels ii 13

The House That Moved 14

Grandpa's Sycamore Tree 15

In Hildegard's Vineyard 16

On the Wildness of the Soul 18

Epiphany Eve, Thinking of Befana 19

Thinking of Abraham 20

One Night in the Sawtooth Mountains 21

On Trust 22

Turnings 23

Musings on the Cinque Terre 24

Spots of Time 25

For John, Ann, and Liam
Les joies de ma vie

Widenings

Rain-ripples broaden on the pond,
so many—thousands, it seems—
forming, spreading, meeting, merging,
resolving into a larger pattern.

They remind me of Whitman—those ceaselessly
widening circumferences of his, so full of energy,
so boundless in expansion!
And I wonder whether we, too, are ripples on a pond—
our minds,
perhaps our spirits, if you believe in such a thing—
widening out
the way Walt said, the way the pond does
as each droplet joins the swirling dance—
whether we, too, expand and meet and merge,
and if we do—

what then?

Our Stories

A reflection, after seeing Claude Lorrain's The Dismissal of Hagar
at the Alte Pinakothek, Munich

Lorrain's painting was not on my agenda that day,
but it caught me,

> *held me,*
> *and for those few moments—*
> *I don't know how many—*
> *we were one, that scene and I—*

> *Hagar is clutching Ishmael's tiny hand, and I feel*
> *his fingers against my own flesh; we are all*
> *so small, and that desert is so vast,*
> *and I feel again the awful not-knowing—*

Sarah is watching from the window above, and ever so slightly
she smiles, as Abraham's stern finger points the way.
I feel again the tangled, crimson convulsion
of a body and mind in the grip of fear. I feel
how Hagar's back must burn with the sting of Sarah's stare,
as sharp as any sun's ray!
With hers, my eyes are already scanning, searching
that dry land for water to fill the small skin she carries,
or for the sustenance of some succulent plant.
Will she ever dream, I wonder,
of raindrops? or of angels?
or even one angel—its wings spread, perhaps,
disturbing the desert dust—

> *I remember,*
> *and I long to say to her, Hagar,*
> *listen! I know this desert!*
> *I know this story—it is mine,*
> *and yours—*
> *Hagar, listen! There will enough water*
> *and there will be enough food,*
> *and there will be*
> *Angels!*

Melville's Study

After visiting Arrowhead, Pittsfield, Massachusetts

You feel it as soon as you step through the doorway
into Melville's study—the air
carries a different charge, more vibrant
than a moment ago on the other side of that threshold,
as if a strong presence enlivens this room
where he seems, still, to sit, looking across the valley;
he chose this house, this room, I am told,
so that through the window
he could see Mount Greylock,
faithfully offering up every day its inspiration,
its own steadfastness steadying his,
as he waits for the words: synesthetic visions,
worlds beyond the mask;
creator and loom, spinning new worlds out of sea-swirls,
watching as they coalesce into some momentous
Yes!
before the next shape-shift imposes itself.

And—perhaps it is the magnetism of the mountain,
perhaps the electric air—
you feel your own soul stirring,
your own mind starting to ask again
the disorienting questions that must churn
inside him, as he listens, pen in hand, for the burning words
that will say what it is that he sees,
his foot ever upon the treadle.

A Daydream of Geese and Angels

Perhaps
the truth depends on a walk around the lake.
     Wallace Stevens

At first, it was only the sudden spectacle: Geese—
hundreds of them—their raucous *honk! honk! honk!*
slicing straight through the quiet of St. Mary's Lake,
their strong wings flashing against a clear October sky,
their small feet skimming, churning—*troubling!*
waters so placid
only a moment ago.

In single, unbroken motion,
they descended—stirred the waters—rose again
out of sight,

and as St. Mary's settled once more into silent clarity—
     you were there
     walking beside me,
          our thoughts,
          yours and mine,
     forming, rising into awareness almost tangible,

saying, through this quivering,
     this newly split veil,
          the words we could not say
              when both of us had voices.

Emissaries

The cardinal came almost every day that week,
flitting among the leaves of the Japanese maple,
poking about, chirping—always chirping—
every day, brilliant crimson in sunlight,
he sang *pretty birdy pretty birdy*
until I noticed
he was looking straight into my eyes,
holding me in mysterious
holy gaze.

Later, amid all the wondering,

I thought of Viktor Frankl, in the gray Bavarian winter,
rifles and insults striking him as he hacked away
at frozen ground, all the while conversing
with his wife, all that while not knowing
whether she had survived the exterminations,

until, he said,
one trembling bright morning,
a small bird landed on the ground beside him
and looked him
straight in the eye—

Station 6

After seeing Matisse's Stations of the Cross,
La Chappelle du Rosaire de Vence

The Stations are mounted on the back wall of a side chapel,
a matrix of white tiles on which harsh charcoal lines
slash their way upward in continuous motion,
bottom left to upper right,
winding, turning, telling as they go that stark
seamless story, featureless shapes
wending their thorny way from the tribunal
to the tomb,

except
at Station 6–

      Just off center, not quite midway along the journey,
a small cloth interrupts the story's inevitable procession;
it bears a face—the only face with features—
nose, mouth, saddened eyes—
an image
pressed onto the fabric
that had been Veronica's veil.

I wonder sometimes what genius,
what spirit, perhaps,
guided the artist's aging hands. After all,
he could have put the Face of the Divine anywhere,
could have portrayed Veronica's quiet act of compassion
as some unremarkable element in the plot.
    Instead, the image compels us to stop,
compels us to think of such simple
moments of presence,
to consider that piece of cloth,
to feel it burning itself
into heart and mind and memory,
compels us
to consider its questions.

Suite in a Light Key

Reflections after seeing Dali's The Sacrament of the Last Supper,
National Gallery of Art, Washington, D.C.

My father sat on his couch that November,
disarmingly serene,
as if he had forgotten
how quickly days can darken.

I watched, desperate to quiet my demons of despair
as they protested the last rays of the setting sun—
    and then he turned
    ever so slightly,
    and in that instant
    all was changed
    as when a curtain is pulled away
    and a new portrait is revealed,

    for in that shifting of his form against the light,
    I could see, through the picture window behind him,
    through him,
    the dark fingers of the ash tree—
    they were playing along tendons and capillaries,
    among molecules already unhooking,
    in and out of realigning light

and I thought of Dali's boat
sailing straight through Jesus—
there, where He sat at the table,
    photons rearranging,
    fragile flesh resolving
    into translucent pattern,
the twelve hiding their eyes,
the bread already broken,
the wine waiting to be poured,
the words, to be spoken,

even while the light,
as here,
reorders itself,

even as the ash tree sways.

Matters of Light

We are slowed down sound and light waves, a walking bundle
of frequencies tuned into the music of the cosmos, we are souls
dressed up in sacred biochemical garments, and our bodies are the
instruments through which our souls play their music.
Albert Einstein

Perhaps Incarnation
is a matter of quanta
    vibrating
    weaving
into the fabric of a body
a pattern of geometries
    color
    texture
    design
absorbed, absorbing,
vertical and horizontal
    threads
    intercrossing,

        Light to light
        Dust to dust
        Spirit to spirit

opposites attracting meeting merging
    then—dancing!
    electric streams coursing
    through veins
    swirls of ever-changing
    ecstasies,
    free forms meeting
    joining
    separating
    creating—
all on their way to fill a heart
so that it can be emptied
    in perpetual cycles

kaleidoscopic fantasies
flowing
around
dark
silent
Centers.

So then,
perhaps death

is an unravelling—

threads
  uncrossing,
        one
           by
              one,

matter
  realigning,
        revealing

      a new

      appearance, a new quality

      of light:

            Dust
                  to
                        dust,

            light
                  to
                        Light!

Convergence

A sudden storm on the turnpike—
Delays—
a priest at the bedside—interrupted—asked
to return, perhaps a little later—and so

Parallel lines—
two belated, now synchronistic arrivals,
the priest's and mine,
he, bearing the sanctified body and blood
and so many hollowed out words,
I bearing the unspeakable understanding:
Last Supper.

Later, into the night around the bed, we had the telling of stories,
old and recent, of songs in four-part harmony,
of jokes played, laughter new and poignant;
then the recounting of this day:

two delays—
parallel lines bend, then
intersect—then
timing suddenly transformed
sanctified!

Call it coincidence, if you must,
or call it convergence,
as when quantum waves suddenly meet in some particulate
instant,
or when a thin veil parts ever so slightly,
and in that moment, for only an instant,
you embrace the exquisite Gift!

Time Travels i

Sometimes I find myself
thumbing through faded photographs:
women in dresses that reach to their laced-up shoes,
men wearing grey fedoras and leaning on canes:
my ancestors, whether I knew them or not.

I wonder about their stories,
about what they learned of wisdom,
and where lie the connections between our lives,
theirs and mine,
and how it is that I know so little of them
and how it is they feel so elusive
and how it is they feel so near.

Time Travels ii

Some evenings, I take books off the shelf, and
I thumb through them, too:
the King James Bible, the Upanishads, the Bhagavad-Gita—
I try to recall the mythologies they taught me
and the stories they still tell, the mysteries they unfold
and the secrets we cannot understand;
          but always, of course, there is the poetry—
Whitman and Eliot, Rumi and Rilke and Oliver—
their music and their rhythms
walk with me through ever-shortening days and
watch with me through dark nights;
and they feel, somehow, the truest of all,
speaking as they do of beauty,
whether I see it or not; and of goodness, surely—
can I not feel it
in a thousand ways and words?
and are these companions not my kin?
and are they not
enough?

The House That Moved

We watched from the old metal glider on the front porch,
Grandpa and I,
caught in the miracle unfolding before our eyes,
scarcely breathing, lest the slightest movement
disturb this unthinkable scene:

> A house,
> its furnishings and figurines left in their precarious places,
> was moving slowly, almost imperceptibly, down the street,
> past our house, past the intersection, past four more houses
> to its new address in the next block,
> where an especially prepared foundation waited
> as if it were quite ordinary for an entire house
> to be simply deposited, in one piece, in some other location.

"Would you look at that," Grandpa whispered as the house crept by.
I nodded, silently summoning all the power I could conceive,
intensely willing that house to hold together—please hold together!
those breakables not to break, those walls not to warp and bend—
please—
faith desperately seeking a place, there
next to the fear.

I think about that day often and about the intense,
singular *willing* that consumed my child's mind in those moments,
and somehow, on that day at least,
played out exactly as I had willed it;
I consider sometimes
how easy prayer seemed
back then.

Grandpa's Sycamore Tree

When I was a young girl, six or so,
the majestic sycamore tree at the end of Grandpa's long back yard
was my sanctuary, long before I knew that word.
 Beneath its dense and spreading leaves,
 settled against its massive trunk,

  I would linger
  listening and watching—
  for that great canopy sheltered
  song birds and angels!
I could hear their music,
see their shadows,
as they sang and frolicked and danced—
and this—
one day
I saw an orb, a great, green, translucent sphere!
  It was bouncing among the branches,
   shape-shifting,
    expanding—
     breathing!
and then
  it stretched itself out so that it seemed as if
   the electric air between us enveloped
    in warmth and sheer beauty
     the tree—and me!

Now, all these years later,
Grandpa's house and the sycamore tree are gone,
buried under concrete and steel.
I think of that holy place often and try to understand
its enduring gift, and I wonder sometimes
where the birds sing now
and where they angels have gone
  and what about
  that shining green sphere—

In Hildegard's Vineyard

O viriditas digiti Dei…!
    Hildegard von Bingen, Symphonia armonia celestium
    revelationum

The Abbey of Hildegard is a majestic merging,
old stones and summer roses;
she keeps watch over Rüdesheim,
and down her hillside,
row upon row,
through the centuries since the first Roman plantings,
ancient vines have delineated
dusty paths to the Rhine.

I linger among the greenness—
    it feels strangely familiar, like home—
and hear the voices of the sisters, singing
glorious melodies!
    O Viriditas digiti dei!

Perhaps it is the purity of the notes,
perhaps the breeze playing among the vines,
but for a moment,
I almost think I see her walking here,
hands on her head, trying to capture some vision—
    All those angels!
    Mandalas full of them!
        circling,
        even as the compositions fall into focus—
and I hear again
    Viriditas!

    See!
    How those tender tendrils extend,
    embrace one another!
    Listen!
    How music surrounds us—
    becomes us—

becomes
such verdant,
such exquisite
life!

On the Wildness of the Soul

Behind the altar at Cologne Cathedral,
a dazzling gold reliquary
startles the senses in sudden chiaroscuro;
it is said to hold the bones of the Magi—
logic tells me otherwise.

And yet,

I am here, finding myself in their story, and—
   perhaps it is all this light—
I hear Pascal—
Le coeur, he whispers,
it has its reasons.

    At length, I begin to make my solitary way
along the cathedral's dark-stone aisles
back into the dimness;
I have scribbled no petition, lit no candle—
what would I say, or pray?

      That I long to know what hot words
      must have burned in those hearts
      to make them so wildly follow a star?

      That I yearn for the wisdom that taught them
      how to heart-listen?

      That sometimes on clear nights,
      I go outside, scan the night sky,
      and wonder—

Epiphany Eve, Thinking of La Befana

I understand why you did not go with them,
those three enigmatic men, obsessed as they were
with finding a Child
in a cradle
somewhere
beneath that bright star.

Ah, but you had dishes to wash,
dusty floors to clean,
and I understand how it is
with dishes and dust and duty;

but who of us has not felt that chill,
that hollowness in the heart,
when soul-stirring is gathered up
and swept away,
when some star,
long since gone from view,
still
burns?

Thinking of Abraham

Story has it that one night Abraham saw
a sky full of stars—

What a night that must have been,
so full as it was of outrageous promise,
vast progeny, he was assured,
as many as the uncountable stars!

He had no child at the time,
yet he believed—
and I imagine his old heart must have quickened
at so grand a thought!

I wonder—
Can he see now, do you think? Across the millennia,
those stars—all those children,
light after light
birthing, dividing, destroying,
burning out—
burning?

I don't know whether such things as time travel are real—
we know so little of our own minds—
whether, centuries from now, any of us could look back
from one point in our human stories to another,
see some thread, some pattern,
see, perhaps,
what has come of us.

But if we can,
if Abraham can,
I wonder what our hearts will feel
then—

One Night in the Sawtooth Mountains

The night sky drew me
into its three-dimensional splendor,
vibrant and unfathomable;
I felt the tingling power of connectedness
on my skin and in my blood, and my mind was
aflame with the beauty of this world
immanently around and deeply within.

Through the window of my little tent there in the mountains,
as I gazed at the stars, and as the gap between us lessened,
    suddenly I was there among them,
        a figure defined by the purity of space,
            dependent on it for my being
            and my autonomy.

Sometimes even now on clear nights,
I can go out under the stars and feel again
    the encircling, embracing energy,
        feel for a moment, in some sudden, subtle space,
            the impossibility of doubt, of fear,
                for I remember
I have been here before,
here where dust and stardust swirl,
unfettered and inextricably connected,
united in this holy, creative moment

            where the Eternal
            still says, *This!*
            Yes! This—!

On Trust

Orion has come round again in the evening sky;
    his three-jeweled belt,
        his long-arching limbs—

they comfort, somehow:
    perhaps it is the faithfulness of his return,
        the presence of his lights;

even when clouds shape-shift between us,
    even when they obscure him utterly
        and I can only believe,
            perhaps trust,

        he is still striding strong,
            across the dark skies;
                sometimes he is

the resurrected Osiris
    out there in his constellated chariot,
        dispensing dreams

and songs; and sometimes,
    I even fancy I can hear him singing—

    Watch and listen—the lyrics go—*Watch*
    and listen—

    whether you see me or not,
      whether you

    remember me
      or not—

Turnings

Summer has been noisy this year,
unprecedented, some say,
what with all the cicadas, tymbaling out
their raucous reverberations, and too many sirens
wailing through sun shards and smoke,
and so many
nefarious scowls.

Yet, in this season of Ordinary Time,
ancient mysteries still unfold at every turn,
and unseen, quiet lives attune to the cycles—

Lammas loaves are baked and blessed and broken;
blackberries, uncommonly sweet this year,
flourish among the brambles; and under dry husks
and broad canopies, corn and melons
swell into succulence; Clare still walks among
those dusty Umbrian olive trees; Bartholomew
prints his books and raises a pint to us all; and Mary,
right on schedule, assumes again her place in heaven;

and even as the first yellowing leaves
break free from the sweet gum, to waft
and sway and dance and descend
to the season of settling in;

even as the shifting slants of light
confirm Earth's faithful turning,
and Sirius returns to nighttime skies—
oh, how I shall look for him there!—

even as unnerving commotion clamors on—

like Persephone, I go about, as each of us must,
gathering seeds for the journey.

Musings on the Cinque Terre

This is no country for an old woman, I fear;
its steep, rocky trails, its cracked, stony steps,
its unrelenting summer sun.
     I step aside to let the younger ones pass;
their strong, tanned legs conquer the craggy trail
without the slightest hesitation,
and the distance widening between us
burns into my bones and

takes hold of my mind—oh, how easily!
I stop and sit for a while in a small
circle of shade
and look toward the sea—

Il mar Ligure is peaceful today,
and at the far edge of its glistening surface,
the horizon is a single thread
of some deep blue veil, a mystical
meeting place of earth-sea and sky—

     I lean against a slender tree,
          breathe—more deeply now—
               consider this outrageous seduction—

Oh, wily quickener of old hearts!

Oh, beguiling whisperer!

Oh! wild odyssean dreams!

Spots of Time

a sudden silence, then the enveloping translucence
before the crash, the unlikely
timing

the inarticulate heard in wordless knowing

a wisp of light pulsating
fleeting
in a pivotal moment

particles entangled
waves formed and reformed
exquisite precision in the gravitational pull

a pillar of light,
soft and loving,
even on a night
of numb dismay

the sublime power of a Mozart horn concerto to transport
mind and spirit to some other continuum, some dimension
where there is only
the truth of the music

that filament, rising like the soul itself
from the dark velvet depths of O'Keeffe's
jack-in-the-pulpit, enlivening heart and mind,
technical perfection and ingenious juxtaposition,
yes, but more than that: it is
beauty and goodness infusing and uniting
in one radiant moment
creator and creation and perceiver

trees in community and communication
whole forests of them
relying on each other

     the intelligence of cells in mortal bodies, knowing
     to be heart cells and not skin cells
     or bone cells or brain or blood, ligament or sinew

     always, the reminder that the geese bring—

Oh, these, and so much more!

No, I do not understand Nature or life or God in the least—
the strange intricacies, the vagaries,
the ways it all swirls and spirals and sometimes dances together
and sometimes careens and crashes, the ways it can
stop me in my tracks
with its horrors
and its beauties
and its enigmas;

     I have felt the anguish of Arjuna's dilemma,
stared into Goliath eyes,
feared as my sluggish feet sank in miry clay,
wrestled with my share of angels, felt the splitting of a heart,
despaired as a once-familiar world utterly dissolved;
such it is said, is the stuff of life; and yet
I see these now as lesser truths,

     for I have learned from Wordsworth:
     there are in our lives spots of time,
     defying logic, transforming life itself;
     they are surely all around us
     and surely dwell within us,

     for how easily and unexpectedly they slip
     into our consciousness!

And then—*oh!*

Oh, what it is
to be held
in such wonder!

Jonel Sallee is a lifelong lover of learning. Her formal education includes a bachelor's degree in English and Humanities (University of Louisville), a master's degree in English (Brown University), and a doctorate in English (University of Kentucky). She spent more than forty years teaching English and Arts and Humanities at the middle school, high school, and university levels in Providence, Rhode Island, and in Louisville and Lexington, Kentucky. Her writings during the years spent in university teaching consisted mainly of scholarly essays on interdisciplinary relationships among literature, philosophy, and science, particularly as these disciplines have found expression in the work of Emerson, Whitman, T. S. Eliot, and Werner Heisenberg.

More recently, her writing interests have turned to poetry. Thanks to an award from the National Endowment for the Humanities to study Mozart's work in Vienna, Austria, she became a lover of travel and subsequently spent as many summers as possible exploring her ancestral, literary, and spiritual roots in Europe. Journals, photos, and memories from those trips are providing much of the inspiration for her current writings. She has previously published poetry in several anthologies and in two chapbooks, *Trees Stand Tall* (Whippoorwill Press) and *Dimensions* (Workhorse).